Blue He
New

Edited by Lorne Shirinian

Other Books from Blue Heron Press

History of Armenia and Other Fiction, short stories by Lorne Shirinian

Rough Landing, poetry by Lorne Shirinian

Blue Heron Press Anthology:
New Voices from Kingston

Edited by Lorne Shirinian

Blue Heron Press,
Kingston, Ontario, Canada

Blue Heron Press Anthology: New Voices from Kingston first edition, Blue Heron Press, 160 Greenlees Drive, Kingston, Ontario, Canada K7K 6P4

Winter Poems, "In Flight," "Winter Comes to the Amey Road," "January's Trail," "Land of Winter's Moon," Northeast Passage: Passamaquoddy Poems, "Summer Passes," "Things Slip Away," "Places in the Night," "Whales and Whale Watchers" ©Tom Vincent, 2000

"Survival," "Retribution," "Winter," and "Crow" © P. S. Sri, 2000

"The Green Man," "Haley Goes for a Swim," "Poems Local, Long and Green," "Cedar Lake Rocks," "Nobody Leaves Here: Musings Upon the BST (Blue Skies Timewarp)" ©Michael Hurley, 2000

"Hide and Seek," "Extras," "Labyrinth," "Headlong Fall," and "The Door Ajar" ©Lorne Shirinian, 2000

All rights reserved. This book may not be produced in whole or in part in any form without permission.

Canadian Cataloguing in Publication Data

Main entry under title:

Blue Heron Press anthology: new voices from Kingston

ISBN 0-920266-20-7

1. Canadian poetry (English) — Ontario — Kingston.*
2. Canadian poetry (English) — 20th century.*
3. Short Stories, Canadian (English) — Ontario — Kingston.*
4. Canadian fiction (English) — 20th century.*
I. Shirinian, Lorne, 1945- .

PS8257.K47B58 2000   C810.8'0971372   C99-932929-4

For Nora, Jagada, Nancy & Noémi

Table of Contents

Introductions

Tom Vincent, 1
    FRONTENAC AXIS
    Winter Poems
        In Flight, 5
        Winter Comes to the Amey Road, 7
        January's Trail, 10
        Land of Winter's Moon, 12

    NORTHEAST PASSAGE
    Passamaquoddy Poems
        Summer Passes, 17
        Things Slip Away, 18
        Places in the Night, 20
        Whales and Whale Watchers, 22

P. S. Sri, 25
    Survival, 29
    Retribution, 38
    Winter, 46
    Crow, 47

Michael Hurley, 49
    Poems Local, Long and Green, 53
        The Green Man, 54
        Haley Goes for a Swim, 57
        Cedar Lake Rocks, 63
        Nobody Leaves Here: Musings Upon
        The BST (Blue Skies Timewarp), 76

Lorne Shirinian, 87
    Hide and Seek, 91
    Extras, 97
    Labyrinth, 107
    Headlong Fall, 108
    The Door Ajar, 109

INTRODUCTIONS

"Winter Poems" are taken from a larger work still in progress entitled *Frontenac Axis / Appalachian Way*. The work is rooted in the geography, geology, and imagery of the Canadian Shield and the northern part of the Appalachian Range, but it explores that terrain more as an imaginative landscape than a literal one. When the arbitrary and accidental definitions and boundaries imposed by political and social history are stripped away, the world of eastern North America emerges as something quite magic, open and free, unconfined by reason and science. It is the mythic potential of this terrain that the poetry pursues. The "Passamaquoddy Poems" are early pieces in what may be a similar effort focused around the Gulf of Maine, the other really magic place in eastern America. There, when the sun comes out of the sea (as it always has) or slips down behind the hills (as it always has), its oblique light sometimes allows you to see the kind of magic I'm taking about.

Tom Vincent

> 'The time has come,' the Walrus said,
> 'To talk of many things:
> Of shoes—and ships—and sealing wax—
> Of cabbages—and kings—
> And why the sea is boiling hot—
> And whether pigs have wings.'
>
> Lewis Carroll, *Through the Looking Glass.*

When the creative impulse grabs you by the throat, you must speak. You need to raise your voice in story and song. You want to express your fears and hopes. You yearn to shape your agonies and ecstasies into striking metaphors and potent symbols. You believe your spoken words will have the power to move. You wish the miracle of communication will set you free. Above all, you hope your fresh-found voice will not get lost in the wilderness.

P. S. Sri

As our cover suggests, the four of us come together here as one to present distinct yet interconnected forays into poetic terrain. We have in common a passion for words, images & rhythms, as well as a common site for our more professional activities: the Royal Military College of Canada, a locale not always considered synonymous with poetic endeavour or promise. Chalk up another first for the Millennium.

It isn't exactly that cadets or DND—to vary Yeats—have come to bring four of their English Dept. profs metaphors for poetry (though this has been known to happen). Rather, we find ourselves both teaching and writing poetry & prose under the same roof, as well as enjoying each other's company, and herein take the opportunity to broaden and deepen this acquaintance. In these pages, we extend this opportunity to you as well, that we may all get to know just a little bit more about how words cut loose, play, dance and—dare we say it?—"fall into position." Welcome to Blue Heron country.

Michael Hurley

I like the idea of this project: four colleagues, four friends, four professors and four writers, each with a very different field of interest, perspective and voice, coming together to share the joy, the sadness and the mystery of our lives. For the past several months, I could see this book happening. As we all live in close proximity in the same hallway at RMC, every day I saw us getting it down for the book: Tom leaning back in his old chair, eyes closed, dreaming new images that taste of rock, soil, and the sea, Sri his door ajar, seated before his computer, intently working on refining his characters, Michael pen in hand pushing the language and images into new rhythms. Here, then, are our words.

Lorne Shirinian

TOM VINCENT

TOM VINCENT

Tom Vincent was born at Fredericton, New Brunswick, in the heart of the Saint John River Valley, in 1943, and grew up in the Annapolis Valley at Clementsport and Windsor, Nova Scotia. In the 1950s in rural Maritime Canada, the rhythms of nineteenth-century life still lingered. Growing up there was something of a Wordsworthian childhood in which the natural world became the most important classroom. Tom's more formal education came from his experiences as a day-student at King's College School, Windsor, an Anglican boys-school modeled on English public schools with a curriculum emphasizing literature, classics, philosophy, theology, and sports. In 1960, Tom entered the University of King's College, Halifax, where he studied English Literature. He came to Queen's University, Kingston, in 1965 to pursue graduate studies in English and joined the staff of the English Department at the Royal Military College in 1969.

The poems printed here come from experiences rooted in the two most prominent literal/imaginative landscapes in Tom's work: Eastern Ontario and Maritime Canada. In both cases, the landscape offers a terrain that has mythic qualities beneath its objective presence, and the poetry attempts to explore those mythic possibilities.

FRONTENAC AXIS

Winter Poems

IN FLIGHT

all day
the light
from the dead
november sky
stripped
the landscape
of its colour
and burdened the air
with the expectation
of colder
wetter winds
sweeping up
through the grim gullies
to fill
the empty branches
with the brittle foliage of winter

late in the day
the sun broke through
ten minutes above the horizon
spilling the thick amber
of its last light
across the stony ridges
and into the brown
bent grasses
that mocked
the memory of summer
along the eastern margin

of this drowned land
between the hills

in the incipient revelations
of the moment
before darkness
erased
the promise of tomorrow
a mated pair of wild ducks
flew across my line of vision
and caught the waning light
on wings
driven by an urgency
that only fear
could admire

WINTER COMES
TO THE AMEY ROAD

the old road bends here
and runs up the hill
to open ground
up through spindles of sumac and thorn
to where
the farmhouse stood
behind split rail fences
among a cluster of out buildings
all gone now
more than eighty years past

today the snow
falling
into this ghost of a roadway
reveals traces of old wagon tracks
scars smoothed by time and weather
into gentle undulations
where the grey shadows
cast by washed out winter skies
pool and spill away
into the premature darkness

the light fading
blurs the features of common day
suspends the sense of time

8 Tom Vincent

and draws imagination
beyond this place
into an age of risk
and struggle
where hardship elevates
perceptions of ancestral dignity

in the emotion of the moment
enthusiasm
obscures the bleak history
of blind purpose
and pernicious self-interest
that stripped the white pines
from these dark mysterious hills
and blew the sides off flowered ridges
in search of phosphates
feldspars
and commercial mica

they settled nothing
these men
blunting their axes
spades
plows
in acts of despoliation
driven
by the loose morality of survival

in the end
they emerged
less than heroic
narrow and callous
at times even malevolent
their fields
and homesteads
outposts of a rapacious people
bent on shaping a desire
for personal fortune
into the guise of a nation

in the pursuit of such pragmatic destinies
they cut this road
into the history
of an unimaginable land
and never understood
the real nature of their losses
before they abandoned it
to time
and winter

JANUARY'S TRAIL

in this forest of sticks
the January sun etches sharp
each twig and needle
against the texture
of the crusted snow

across my path
the footprints
of mice
and rabbits and partridge
dance among the spear points
where deer hooves
cut to the frozen ground

gone hours past
hidden now
deep in holes
and under boughs
they wait the blast of winter
and startle
at the sound of my footfalls

I think of them
warm and safe

a child's book vision of nature
like the time
I curled up
among the blueberries
and the tea berries
to sleep
in the afternoon sun
protected by August
and the breath
of other unseen deities

I do not remember
what sins were whispered
in my ear

but when I awoke
I found myself
here

LAND OF WINTER'S MOON

there is a wilderness
I have in mind
that lies
beyond the winter moon
but I am waiting
for a time
afraid
I should begin
too soon

it is the skeleton
of that land
I wish to see

a vision
of its bones

laid out
smooth and gentle
under the covering
of the first snow fall

O let me first
at a distance
see it
by the cold light
of winter's night

late
in the dark dance
of the hills

when out of the pine groves
the shadows whirl
the shadows spin
across the open ridges
and into the waste
of ponds
and ditches
that shape the nether side
of this blind world

O let me first
by starlight
bright
enter in

when the winter owls
in white
sweep down
the long ravines

contaminating the silver meadows
with fear
on silent wings
and spreading death
on talons
black as sin
while the faint hearted shiver
in their skin

O let me
come to it
alone

before the first sun rises
before the first sun devises
appropriate cruelties
to rend
the seamless sensuality
that binds
this seductive landscape
innocent of all design

lying quiet
in the comfort of the morning
as light advances
and dreams decline

there is a wilderness
I have in mind
that lies
beyond the winter moon
but I am waiting
for a time
afraid
I should begin
too soon

NORTHEAST PASSAGE

Passamaquoddy Poems

SUMMER PASSES

St. Andrews, New Brunswick

Watch
along the sea
and down among the granite

watch
along the margins
of the bay

watch
among the rushes

watch
where the waves say

hush
hush

THINGS SLIP AWAY

the tide
this morning
offers little comfort
lies
herring barren
ebbed
and quiet

over the channel
an osprey
hovers
stubborn against the wind
trading instinct and energy
against a catch
that does not come

whatever sense of gain
the first light might have offered
has gone away
leaving only
a litter of broken mussel
and clam shell
to mark its retreat

and a severed arm
the remains of a crab
lies stiff on the sand

where indifferent forces
tossed it
before disappearing
into the shadows that linger
after the sun
has fashioned the day
in its own image

PLACES IN THE NIGHT

at night
seabirds are silent
gone to islands
where darkness
and the evening fog
muffle their anxieties

under the weight of night
their murmurings
are soothed
submerged in the undertones
that shape the foundations
of the coming tide

above the sound of waters rising
over the fields of kelp
the bell buoy calls
from the harbour mouth
insistent in its repetition
that all is well with the night
that safe passage lies
though darkened channels
out to the open sea

but even the foolish know
that there are mysteries

too deep to measure
places in the night
that lie
beyond Letete
and past The Wolves

places
where there is no distinction
between ocean and sky

where seabirds are struck dumb
by the enormous
emptiness that opens
before their startled eyes
erasing
all the promises
that went before

WHALES
AND WHALE WATCHERS

i

wind and sea along this coast
conspire against the sun
waves do not hold their edge
nor rocks their warmth

summer days lie
light on the hills
drawing the eye away
from the darker purposes at play
in the slow currents circling
the Gulf of Maine

on charts
this corner of the ocean appears
innocuous enough
its lines of elevation and decline
suggest no great mystery

Georges Bank
Jeffreys Ledge
Isles of Shoals

simple common names
denoting a familiar world
and designed to keep it that way

it is the summer visitors
that bring a sense of dislocation
the whales
and the whale watchers

ii

the latter come and go quickly
more nuisance than threat
it is the whales
that are the problem

their passage through these waters
speaks of greater depths
and darknesses
beyond our understanding

it shakes something loose
in imagination
in memory

and in the presence of those grey forms rising
we are filled with unfamiliar fear
an instinctive understanding that this moment
and our knowledge of its meaning
will slip away
will disappear
before we fully comprehend
its nature and its purpose here

iii

in the long hours after the whales
and the whale watchers have gone
the coast waits

not for their return
but for a visitation from the dark cruelties
that haunt the whale's path

and in the rising furies of the winter gale
driving headlong against the seaward hills
we will hear the sound of anger
 and see malice made articulate
in water against stone

and we will not know
if it is we they seek
or whether this rage comes
from having once again
missed the primary quarry

P. S. SRI

P. S. SRI

Dr. P.S.SRI—a Canadian of Indian origin—hails from Chennai (Madras), the capital of Tamil Nadu, India. Currently, Sri is a Professor of Comparative Literature in the Dept. of English at Royal Military College, Kingston, Ontario. From 1985 to 1995, Sri taught Literature and Philosophy at Royal Roads Military College, Victoria, B.C. Sri's research is wide-ranging and includes East-West Literary and Philosophical ideo-synthesis, Post-colonial and Multicultural Commonwealth Literature, Arabic and Persian Literature as well as Sanskrit and Tamil Literature. Sri is the author of a critical work entitled *T.S.Eliot, Vedanta and Buddhism* (Vancouver: University of British Columbia, 1985). Sri has also published articles on Bharati Mukherjee, Margaret Laurence, W.B.Yeats, T.S.Eliot, E.M.Forster, Rumi, Sanskrit myth, Tamil literature and folklore. Sri has received many awards, including the Canadian Federation of Humanities Grant (1984-85), the Social Sciences and Humanities Research Council Grant (1990-91). In 1991, Sri won a prize in an International Essay Contest organized by Washington and Jefferson College, Pennsylvania, USA. In 1993, Sri was awarded the first National Prize for Canada by UNESCO in an International Literary Competition commemorating the 500th Anniversary of Columbus' discovery of the New World. In 1996-97, Sri received a prestigious research grant through the Women and Development program of the Shastri Indo-Canadian Institute at the University of Calgary.

As an international citizen, Sri feels that all things human and non-human deserve respectful attention. The short stories and poems that follow are semi-autobiographical and partially mirror Sri's experiences under a Canadian sky.

SURVIVAL

She woke up in the dark, a cockroach in her mouth. She retched violently and spat out the squirming insect noisily. She groped under her bed for her sandals. At once, numerous cockroaches, large and small, scrambled up her right hand and swarmed all over her body. One ran over her shoulder into her right ear. Another shot up her chest onto her face and tickled her nostril with its moustache. Still another raced down her stomach and got entangled in the matted hair around her vulva.

She leapt out of her bed, plucked the sticky creatures from her ear, nose and crotch and flung them away in disgust. Sweeping her arms in front, she fumbled for the bedside lamp. In her sleep-befuddled state, she found it difficult to orient herself in the darkened room. She banged her right knee hard against the leg of a chair and fell headlong on the uncarpeted floor. Instantly, an army of cockroaches invaded the nooks and crannies of her body. She fought them off vigorously and simultaneously tried to regain her feet.

The pain in her knee combined with her distress over the cockroaches dispelled the lingering mists of sleep. Gradually, her thoughts cleared and she recollected what and where she was—a down-and-out immigrant Indian woman looking desperately for a job in WASPish Toronto. Only this morning she had moved into this dirt-cheap cockroach-infested hellhole of a room on the outskirts of Scarborough.

She slipped on the slimy bodies of several cockroaches

and fell heavily to the floor. Cockroaches of every imaginable size—huge, tiny, fat, thin, long, short—all inexpressibly hairy and filthy seemed to pounce on her in the dark, and drive her insane.

She swore. With a forceful push of her hands, she managed to get up on her feet. She thrashed about the strange room, cracking her shins and bruising her arms on jutting pieces of furniture. She peered fixedly at the gloom that surrounded her, trying vainly to grope her way to the light switch near the door. But she had lost her sense of direction when she fell and she couldn't tell where the door was in the darkness.

As she stood there, collecting her scattered wits, her twenty-five-year-old past flashed swiftly before her mind's eye.... *her lower middle class Brahmin background in Madras on the southeast coast of India facing the Bay of Bengal... her father's death when she was still in primary school... her mother's heroic self-sacrifice in bringing her up single-handedly by backbreaking labour as a cook... the years of impoverishment, deprivation and semi-starvation... her progress through high school and college sustained solely by the miracle of merit scholarships... her quixotic decision to major in English Literature instead of in job-oriented Physics or Engineering... her mother's proud tears over her brilliant performance in the M.A. examinations... her own pleasure at her unprecedented A+ and university first rank... her frustration over prolonged unemployment... her anger when she faced discrimination in college after college for having come into this world a Brahmin... her surprise and delight when out of the blue a research fellowship from a Canadian university descended upon her...*

With a whirr of diaphanous wings, a cockroach collided with her face. Startled, she clapped her hand to her forehead, caught the wriggling insect between her fingers and cast it away. But already a number of other cockroaches were clambering over her thighs, creeping down her spine, crawling up her shoulders, landing on her hair and eyelids. She plied her arms and legs energetically, but failed to dislodge all the unwelcome invaders. As she whirled about madly, the darkness that pressed on her from every side suddenly assumed the monstrous shape of a gigantic cockroach. She panicked . . .

*On arrival in Toronto in the fall, she had learnt to her dismay that her Indian degree wasn't considered good enough and that she was required to repeat her M.A. before enrolling in the doctoral program. She had stormed into the Chairman's office with her fiery questions. Why hadn't she been informed prior to her departure from Madras? Why had she been lured halfway across the world by false promises? There had been no satisfactory answer. The Chairman—preoccupied with his upcoming book—***Compassion in the Poetry of Wordsworth***—had dismissed her predicament as an unfortunate oversight. She had debated whether she should return home. She had very little money, however. She would have to save part of her monthly allowance from her fellowship for quite some time for her return passage. She had swallowed her pride, therefore, and silently bent to her task. For seemingly endless months, she had trekked from her lonely basement room in the graduate students' residence to her lectures and led a mole-like existence among the library stacks. Often, she'd felt friendless and alone. Most of the things her fellow Canadian students took for granted she'd found strange, confusing and even frightening—skating, skiing, dating, partying, drinking, driving. Her head had reeled under the impact of new and even vulgar terms—"getting stoned", "smoking grass", "bull-shit", "asshole" and "fuck". Her Brahminical soul had shrunk back from the abyss of free love and casual sex. Food especially had been an insurmountable problem at first. Stubborn vegetarian that she was, she had felt she'd starve to death in this land of steaks and sausages, hamburgers and hot dogs. After a couple of months' steady diet of lettuce and coleslaw, carrots and peas, bread and milk, she had feared* she'd turn into a rabbit. Just in time, she had discovered pizzas and pancakes, spaghetti and quiche. And eventually, after burning her fingers and almost setting fire to her clothes, she had learnt to cook rice and **sambar** in the common kitchen at McKay Hall. Winter had been another ordeal. In November, the weather had turned cold. She had muffled herself up in a heavy winter coat, gloves and winter boots and had learnt to dread the wind chill factor. The beauty of snow-clad bushes and trees glistening in the sun had taken her breath away, even as she had slipped on the icy sidewalks, sprained her ankle and cursed. But she had held on grimly and succeeded. She had completed her two-year M.A. program with distinction in about a year and a half. That spring the world had smiled and hope had sprouted in her heart... only to be blighted when she was told she couldn't be given a scholarship for the Ph.D. program because of a shortage in government funding. It was too late to apply elsewhere that year.

"A temporary setback," she told herself. "I'll work somewhere and make some money. Next year, I can continue my studies."

Easier said than done.

"You only taught part-time during your M.A. program. So you can only claim partial unemployment insurance," said the unctuous officer in Manpower.

"Sorry we can't hire you, but you lack Canadian experience, you know," whispered the Personnel Manager in Advanced Education, stretching her thin lips in a smile.

"Sure, we could use someone like you, but you aren't familiar with our Canadian jargon, are you? Oh yeah, we can train you, but it's too much of a hassle. Can't go back to India, eh?" burbled the jolly little bald News Editor of the **Star**, patting his beer belly fondly.

"If only you were white, I'd hire you on the spot, but brownies are bad for customer relations."

The icy voices laid down the law and brooked no argument. Her *soul a-quiver, but grim-faced and tight-lipped, she had persisted in her quest...*

She drew in her breath in deep lungfuls and tried to steady her nerves. "My mind's playing tricks," she chided herself, "conjuring up phantoms, making monsters out of mere insects." She forced her flesh to tolerate the repulsive feel of countless creepy cockroaches and concentrated her thoughts on reaching the door. Palms extended, she advanced her feet ever so slowly in front of her in the inky blackness, taking care not to stumble against the bed or collide with a side table. Minute by minute, her eyes were becoming more sensitive to varying shades of darkness, so that she was able to espy a thin strip of grey in the far corner where a faint light from the passage struggled to peep in under the door. Ignoring what seemed a slimy battalion of cockroaches that marched all over her body, hid in her armpits, flew into her hair and perched on her eyelids, she grit her teeth and groped for the light. Her hair itched abominably, her skin crawled with unspeakable disgust, her eyes smarted from sweat. As she inched forward, the floor seemed to be alive with cockroaches that scurried under her feet and tripped her. Twice, she fell down heavily. At long last, when she thought she'd go berserk under the onslaught of the cockroaches, her hands grasped the door. With a sob of relief, she twisted the door knob with her right hand and flung the door open. Simultaneously, she found the control panel beside the door and threw the switch.

She had plodded vainly from door to door in Toronto looking for a job. Her warm optimism had gradually cooled. She had soon become expert at spotting trouble at a glance. In time, the polite brush-off, the snobbish smile, the racist grimace, the rude finger and the angry fist all alike left her unmoved. Her heart had hardened to icy despair. Her unemployment insurance checks had slowed to a trickle and then stopped and she had been forced to become "a welfare bum."

The other day, she had gone downtown to collect her welfare cheque. She had reluctantly joined a long line of smelly, hairy, loud-mouthed ne'er-do-wells and awaited her turn quietly. After what had seemed an eternity of pushing, panting and swearing, she had finally been thrust before a gross fat slug of an officer. At the sight of the officer's gargantuan stomach straining at his pant clasps and oozing fish-belly white through the gaps in his shirt, she had found it hard to suppress a grin. With an enraged squint, the officer had waved at her impatiently to sign the register before receiving her cheque. She had stooped low to sign her name, when someone had jostled her hard in the back. Losing her balance, she had shot over the edge of the desk and collided heavily with the mountainous folds of flesh in front of her. She had knocked the officer over backward and landed on his ballooning stomach with a resounding thump. After a momentary hush, the room had exploded into laughter. Red-faced and wheezing, the officer had scrambled back on to his feet, hauled her up roughly from the floor and spit in her eyes, blinding her. "How dare you touch me, you brown scum?" the officer had snarled, catching her by the scruff of her neck and throwing her out of the room. She had collapsed in a heap on the floor of the corridor. "Here, take this and get the hell outa here!" the officer had snarled, flinging a cheque in his face. She had no heart to protest. She had got up slowly and wiped the spit off her face with her sleeve. The cheque had fluttered to the ground and she had bent down to pick it up, oblivious to the officer's gloating smile and the deafening catcalls emanating from the room.

As she straightened up, she had noticed the poster on the wall. It had been from the Citizen Actions Committee promising help to all needy persons in finding a job. Obeying an obscure impulse, she had sought out the address on the poster. She had found the Committee in a modest two-storey building in an alley near Yonge Street. To her surprise, three or four women had been in charge, fielding the queries of the few down-and-outers who had drifted in with kindness and tact, scanning the computer sheets piled on their desks and making countless phone calls. She'd been greeted by a plain young blonde in a loose white turtle neck sweater and faded blue jeans. With a compassionate smile, Carol had listened to her tale of woe and sprung into action. She had called several potential employers on her behalf. A couple of them had refused even to interview a Pakie, while others had told her exactly where a curry-smelling brownie could go. Carol's sensitive nose had wrinkled in disgust, but her eyes had lit up with fury and determination. She had let her go that day only after lining up a couple of interviews. She did not get a job that day, but she had found hope.

Encouraged by the spark in Carol's eyes, she had gone back to her day after day. Together, they had waged a tremendous battle for her survival. After a few weeks, her meagre income from welfare had forced her to move early one morning from her comfortable bachelors' suite to the cheapest place she could find in the suburbs. After dumping her bags on the creaky bed in her squalid room, she had set out immediately on her job hunt. Carol had lined up an interview for her around noon at the Association for the Mentally Retarded. Doubts had besieged her: "What does it mean —mentally retarded? Insane? Am I fit only to work with lunatics?" But she had kept her appointment. In her confused state of mind, she could not tell whether she had done well or ill in the interview. On the way home, she had stopped at the Public Library on impulse. For about three hours, she had steeped himself in the literature of mental retardation at the library. She had emerged in the late afternoon sun, deeply ashamed of her ignorant prejudice in equating mental retardation with insanity. She had been particularly impressed by the work of Jean Vanier, the son of a former Governor-General of Canada who had given up a brilliant career in the Navy to found a home called L'Arche outside Paris for the mentally retarded. Vanier's book **Be Not Afraid** *had been an eye-opener. With a profound sense of wonder, she had learnt of the love and joy that prevailed in the lives of the mentally retarded despite their physical shortcomings, of their innocence of sustained deceit and treachery, of their childlike delight in the ordinary* and the commonplace, of their freedom from grasping money-mindedness. She had even begun to yearn for an opportunity to work with the mentally retarded. 'Here is a chance,' she had told herself, "to test my Vedanta, to see if I can overcome my hang-ups and serve Christ in the poor and the handicapped, the unwanted and the unloved, humbly and in self-surrender." On reaching her room, she had seated herself cross-legged on the floor, straightened her spine, closed her eyes and prayed. Her breathing had slowed, her nerves had calmed down and gradually a ray of light had penetrated her gloom. "Am I not short-changing myself by my overactive imagination?" she had asked herself. "Discrimination is not new to me. Have I not faced it in my own motherland? Why should I now feel defeated by racism under an alien sky? Has it not been offset by the warmth and friendliness I have encountered in Carol? Should I not therefore give up my own hang-ups and extend myself in compassionate service to the mentally retarded?" And eventually, ever so slowly, she had felt a warmth in her heart, a surge of love. The ringing of the phone had penetrated her calm. As she picked up the receiver, she had known intuitively she had a good job at last.

The room was flooded with light. She blinked. As her eyes grew used to the sudden brightness, she saw with devastating clarity that her overactive mind had conjured up imaginary monsters in the dark. Only five or six cockroaches were crawling over various parts of her body, while another eight or nine were nestling between the bed clothes and trailing on the floor. Pirouetting rapidly, she flailed her arms and legs wildly, unintentionally executing a comic break dance. One by one, the creepy little creatures dropped to the floor.

Swiftly, she grabbed an issue of *The Globe and Mail* from a side table, furled the magazine into a makeshift insect-basher and brought it down with all her strength on the nearest cockroach and squashed it.

The smug grin on the fat face of the Welfare Officer was wiped out and the poisonous hate that had mushroomed unsuspectedly deep down inside her died quickly.

Her arm rose and fell, rose and fell, again and again and yet again, as she hunted out the fleeing cockroaches and demolished them one by one.

One by one, they died—the patronizing smile, the dirty look, and the lewd remark. One by one, they were vanquished—the polite indifference, the sick joke, the wounding insult, and the violent gesture. One by one, the demons left her - the hurt and the loneliness, the devouring bitterness, the crippling self-pity and the impotent rage.

And she was free.

When she had swept out the dead cockroaches, she walked over to the window, opened the curtains and looked out. Beyond the next hi-rise, she saw the break of dawn.

RETRIBUTION

It was the witching hour of midnight when he reached the ruined farmhouse.

At dusk, he'd gone over to Rachel's home near Lemoine Point. His visit had been so pleasant in the beginning. He'd no idea it would come to such a disastrous end.

The moonless sky had spread a dark mantle everywhere. The undergrowth was so thick he stopped the car a short distance from the abandoned well. He got out, went round and opened the other door. His eyes met the blank staring eyes of Rachel's corpse.

His tongue clove to the roof of his mouth in fear. Apart from the fierce pounding of his heart, the soft whispering of the leaves and the monotonous chirping of the crickets, there was no sound. It was silent as a graveyard.

As he strove desperately to gather his courage, his thoughts flew. Scene by agonizing scene, the events of the past six hours replayed themselves in his mind with such intensity that he actually *relived* them. . . .

Slowly, Raj extricated himself from Rachel's arms, curled round his neck in a sensuous embrace. Displaying her contours with deliberate coquetry, she smiled mischievously.

"You're giving me up, aren't you?," she queried, "now that you're going for a wife?" She encircled him again with her silken arms.

"You know I'm getting married?" He was surprised.
"Only too well," she murmured, caressing his cheek and peering intently into his eyes.

The greenish glow of her eyes held him spellbound and threatened to draw him deep into her coils. With great difficulty, he resisted her enchantment and pulled himself away from her clutches. Carefully avoiding her eyes, he muttered, "Our affair's over, Rachel!"
Instead of recoiling from him, she clasped her arms tighter around his neck. "You must be nuts," she crooned, "if you think you can get rid of me so easily. If you must marry, marry ME!"
Raj laughed. "Are you mad? You're a whore and I'm a well-known doctor. How can we ever get married? I'll lose all respect in the Indian community. Worse, I can't ever hold up my head again among my friends here in Kingston."
Sparks flew from her eyes. "You've been chasing me like a dog in heat for the past two years. Did your pride go fishing then?"
He shrugged. "Guess I was bewitched. Let's come to brass tacks, Rachel, shall we? How much money do you want? I'll pay you whatever you ask. Just don't dream of marrying me!"
Rachel laughed scornfully. "My dear doc," she cried, "you can't wash your hands off me so easily. You'll regret it, I promise you, if you don't marry me."
"You threatening me?" Raj growled. "You don't scare me, you bitch!"
"You should be tickled to death with these photographs then," she screamed, as she swiftly opened a bureau that stood in a corner of the bedroom, grabbed a handful of colour prints and flung them in his face. All the intimacies of their secret life—the ardent kisses, the passionate embraces, the private ecstasies, the forbidden delights—fanned out before his horrified gaze on the tiled floor and mocked him. He stooped quickly to gather and tear them all apart into a thousand little pieces, but hesitated at the sound of Rachel's derisive laughter.
"Do you think I'm cuckoo, Raj?" she asked disdainfully. "Go

ahead and tear them up!" she said. "I don't care as long as the negatives are safe with me!"

He was about to pounce on her, but stopped short at the sudden note of warning in her voice. "You daren't touch me, you fool! she crowed. "If anything happens to me, my lawyer will use the negatives to destroy you."

Fear rooted him to the spot, as Rachel slid gracefully towards him. Raising herself sinuously on her toes, she wound her arms around his neck and kissed him. Her soft breath fanned his cheeks. "Don't worry, Raj!" she murmured enticingly. "Nobody will ever see these photographs or the negatives. I wont betray you, darling! Let's get married and have a wonderful time together. Come, look into this mirror! See for yourself how we're made for each other!" In fact, the mirror on the bedroom wall did show off his handsome brown face and her sensuous golden figure very attractively.

But Raj was in no mood to relish Rachel's intoxicating beauty. He felt cornered and manipulated. Once upon a time, at the beginning of their tempestuous affair, he had fancied Rachel's slender arms were fragrant garlands of flowers. Now, they seemed constricting nooses around his neck. Especially since she was blackmailing him into marriage. He longed to walk away from her, for Rachel could muddy and poison his whole life. Suddenly, a venomous impulse sprouted within him—kill her! But he remembered the negatives and the thought died as quickly as it was born. 'Where could she have hidden the negatives?' he wondered. 'If only I could get hold of them and destroy them and her together,' he reflected wistfully, 'her lawyer would be powerless to hurt me.' Instinctively, he sensed she must have concealed those crucial negatives right here in her bedroom.

"A penny for your thoughts!" Rachel's amused voice abruptly recalled him from his wishful thinking to harsh reality. 'She's bent on marrying me. I must play along with her till I can outsmart her,' he resolved and began to act out his decision immediately. Masking his inner turmoil, he smiled at her fondly.

"Never realized you loved me so much, Rachel! I will marry you!" he promised.

Rachel's face became radiant. She hugged him and kissed him tenderly on the lips. "Oh, Raj!" she gurgled in delight. "We must celebrate. Let me get some champagne!" she cried and danced out of the bedroom.

Except for the muffled echo of her satin slippers down the carpeted staircase, her house was as silent as a grave. They were quite alone, for Rachel had discreetly sent away her maidservant earlier in the evening, anticipating his arrival. The digital clock on the night table beside the queen-size bed flashed eleven. The night was still young for what he had in mind.

The moment her footsteps faded, Raj leaped into action. Fishing out a cigarette lighter from his jacket, he lit it and held the flame close to the bedroom drapes. The flimsy cloth caught fire at once. He tore it down, stamped on it with his shoes and prevented the fire from spreading. At the same time, he shouted, "Fire! Rachel! Fire!"

Rachel came running. She stood still for a moment at the door, startled by the burning cloth and the billowing smoke in the bedroom. The next instant she rushed to the bureau, opened the inner safe, took out a white envelope and stuffed it down between her breasts.

She turned only to collide with Raj. Her surprised cry died in her throat as he clamped his hand down hard on her mouth. She sobbed and struggled as he thrust his free hand into her cleavage, groped and grabbed the envelope she had just secreted away there. Then, he pushed her away from him brutally. She fell down flat on her back, struck her head on the steel bedpost and fainted. Raj didn't waste even a glance on her. He was too busy, tearing open the envelope, inspecting the negatives that fell out in the dim light of the bedroom and making sure they were *indeed the ones he sought. Painstakingly, he picked up every one of the photographs that lay scattered on the tiled floor. He threw them and the negatives into the fire that was still smouldering in a corner. He watched with infinite satisfaction as they were all charred to ashes and then ground out the flames with his heel. With a sigh of relief, he turned and reeled under the fierce onslaught of Rachel, who had by now recovered her senses and figured out that he had tricked her into giving up her precious negatives.*

She clawed at his face in her fury. Fearing she might scratch his eyes out with her sharp red nails, he caught hold of her wrists. She squirmed and struggled. Shifting his grip abruptly to her bare shoulders, he exerted all his strength, forced her to lie back flat on the bed and pinned her down with the full weight of his body.

Inch by inch, his skilled surgeon's hands crept up her smooth tanned shoulders. His slim brown fingers grasped her soft white neck hard and throttled her. Her face turned a dirty red. Her lips flew apart as she gasped for air. The red tip of her tongue protruded from the open cage of her mouth, fluttered rapidly, slowed, and then lolled out. Her hands that beat a sharp tattoo on his chest collapsed at her side. Her life had fled.

He relaxed his stranglehold, shook off her body contemptuously and stood up. The bedside digital clock throbbed in time with his pulse. "Murder!" it signalled. "Run! Run!" it urged him silently. His heart raced. Fighting against the temptation to flee, he forced himself to think calmly.

'Rachel's house is all by itself in this side lane near Bayridge Drive,' he reasoned. 'It's hidden by trees and bushes from the other homes in the neighbourhood. It's unlikely, therefore, that anyone noticed my arrival after dark. So, if I manage to destroy all signs of struggle here and get rid of her body, no one will ever suspect me. Even if they do, in the absence of both the evidence and the body, they would be powerless to act.' His heart-beat slowed down.

'But how can I dispose of this dead body?' he asked himself. His heart began to thump again. Wave upon wave of fear shook his

slender frame, causing torrents of sweat to break out upon his forehead. He wiped his brow clean with his shirt sleeve. Suddenly, he recalled the ruined farmhouse with the abandoned well on the outskirts of the city on the way to Ganonoque. 'Must throw Rachel's body into that well and sink it,' he decided and then plunged into action.

Fetching a vacuum cleaner from a closet in the attached bathroom, he plied it diligently in the corner where the ashes and charred fragments lay in a heap. The floor was free of debris in a trice. He replaced the machine after removing its filter bag. Ripping the bag open, he emptied its contents into the toilet. He tore the bag up, threw the shreds in and flushed the dirty water down the sewer.

Then, he ferreted out a canvas bag, a strong cord and a few bowling balls from the walk-in closet. He flung the balls into the bag and tied it securely with the cord to the feet of the corpse. 'This great bulk is sure to take Rachel down to her final rest on the well-bed,' he chuckled.

Wielding his handkerchief expertly, he wiped all the objects in the bedroom clean of his fingerprints. He rapidly scrutinized every nook and corner of the room to reassure himself that he was not leaving any incriminating evidence behind him.

He heaved the corpse onto his shoulders with a groan. He stumbled downstairs and slipped out through the side door into the garage. Closing the door behind him, he carefully wiped the doorknob free of prints and headed for his car. By the time he reached it, his backbone was cracking, his breath was rasping in his throat and his body was bathed in sweat. Gritting his teeth, he opened the front door of the car and propped up Rachel's body next to the driver's seat.

He turned the key in the ignition and the car purred into life. He inched it out of the garage onto the driveway and turned into the lane. After driving slowly for a few blocks to avoid attention, he quickly turned into the highway and pressed the accelerator down to the floor. The car sped toward the ruined farmhouse. . . .

Collecting his shattered wits with an almost superhuman effort, he turned his back to the corpse, wrapped its stiffening arms round his neck and pulled with all his strength. The corpse emerged slowly out of the car, collapsed heavily on his back and bore him down, so that he could not stand up straight. Straining every nerve and muscle, he staggered toward the well. He had to take only about a hundred steps, but he felt he was creeping along like a snail for eternity.

Gigantic elms brooded over the well. As they swayed in the breeze, they took on the appearance of evil witches shaking their dark locks at him and struck terror into his soul. Some horrible fiend seemed to stalk him and push him toward his nemesis.

When he finally reached his journey's end, he was reeling with exhaustion and fear. Supporting himself on the crumbling edge of the parapet, he peered into the well. Was there any water or not? Prying a pebble loose, he threw it in. Seconds later, he heard a 'plop' followed by a series of 'plops,' as the stone struck the water and set echoes reverberating up and down the well.

He longed to finish his task and run. Hastily, he tried to remove the dead arms draped round his neck. They refused to budge. His heart missed a beat. *Rigor mortis* had set in. He had forgotten it in his extreme anxiety, in spite of being a doctor! Cursing himself for his stupidity, he grasped the leaden body on his back with both his hands and, exerting all his strength, tried to dislodge the corpse and hurl it into the well.

Unexpectedly, his hands slipped. The corpse landed on his back with a thud. The sudden jolt caused the arms to tighten around his wind pipe and strangle him.

He choked. His eyes bulged and threatened to leap out of their sockets. His face contorted in agony. Blindly, he groped for air and dashed his head against the disintegrating wall.

Several pebbles broke loose and sped towards the water. 'Plop, plop, plop'—they sounded. 'Plop, plop, plop'—the echoes replied. For a wild moment, he imagined that Rachel's corpse was mocking him with its grotesque mirth.

He lost his balance and fell headlong into the well. He went under like a stone and swallowed water. He struggled up to the surface and strove to keep his head above the water, but the water forced its way down his nostrils into his lungs. He gagged. Relentlessly, the combined mass of the corpse and of the balls dragged him down to the depths.

In my evil beginning was my vile end... That sardonic thought was his last as his body plummeted to the bottom of the well, the corpse's arms still entwined lovingly around his neck.

WINTER

IS.

Scarce a month ago,
these trees that line the roadside
like sentinels awaiting inspection

> ravished the eye, a riot of colour—
> bright orange and pale yellow,
> a mottled brown, a hectic red.

Now,

the first shiver of ice whistling in the wind
and snow-streamers albino-snaking across the ground,

defenseless and shorn they stand,
bare, gaunt, austere,

stretching forth a myriad skeleton arms to implore

A ghostly withering drapery.

CROW

Perched
   on the edge
      of a ruby-brown, emerald-leaved, wind-weighted,
         tossed hither and thither by the rain
                                              branch,

She broods,
   her darker-than-ebonite wings still, poised,
      in unconscious and involuntary mastery
         of the downward pull of
                                              gravitation.

On the aery unknown—
   undulating before her side-long glance,
      all a-tremble for the feathery feel and caress
         of her soon-to-be
                                              flight.

Suddenly she stiffens,
   as though deep in the recesses of her shadowy mind,
      a thought, long-entertained and half-forgotten,
         had warmed to life in the watery sun,
            flamed and guttered to its
                                              close.

Shifts her weight,
   in deliberate slow-motion,
      from claspéd footing to out-thrust beak,
         flexes wings, draws in her crooked claws and plunges head-first
            into the wind-swept-clean rain-washed-fresh morning
                                              space.

Then soars aloft,
   swifter than an eyelid's soundless blink
      fast shrinks to a sooty speck in the distant blue
         and then by the naked eye is no more to be
                                      discerned.

Behind her,
   the forsaken bough waves to-and-fro
      in frantic seeking of a lost companionship,
         while the close-bred leaves plot together, deal in whispers
            and drown the monotonous lament of the dripping
                                                water

MICHAEL HURLEY

MICHAEL HURLEY

After the usual briefing for the descent, reincarnated en masse in Sixties Seedlings Batch in unsuspecting small-town Ontario (Stompin' Tom's Tillsonburg: "My back still aches..."). Up for a challenge or unprepared from the start, born with umbilical cord wrapped round neck twice etc. Medical consensus up to 12th month: "failure to thrive." And so it goes. Developed humour, verbal wit and word play (such as they are) to defuse violence in public school yard and deflect peer pressure to conform to hive personality in high school. Travelled around planet at 19 (1970)—Canada, Europe, Middle East, Afghanistan, India, Nepal... and back. MA'd at U.W.O. in London. Thanks to Dianna Symonds, energized to this day by poet/playwright James Reaney's "Ontario Literature and Culture" course. Ph.D.'d at Queen's, Kingston. Met Mary McGillivray, Les Monkman and other luminaries there, plus Greg and Gini Forbes and other friends in music-yoga-tai chi-meditation-peace-tofu circles. Met Nancy MacMillan and eventually through her our son Casey (9) and our daughter Elena (6)... and my heart. We live with animals in woods-lake-rock country ideal for Full Catastrophe Living. Taught at Queen's for 4 years 'til phone call outta blue offering job teaching poetry to the military. (You have your karma, I have mine.) Honoured by cadets/faculty with Teaching Excellence Award. U of Toronto publishes my *Borders of Nightmare*—not autobiography but a connect-the-dots between Father of Canlit John Richardson and a cast a 1000s. Still committing random acts of poetry plus readings, cartooning, stand-up comedy, clowning, Men's Group stuff and gratitude (thanks Mom for everything). Currently working on book on Graeme Gibson in concert with other Southern Ontario Gothic writers as well as own poetry collection. Still crazy after all these years.

POEMS LOCAL, LONG AND GREEN

Summer '99 at Cedar Lake, Eastern Ontario, gave birth to these four poems. Their first incarnation was as poster-size colour photocopies incorporating words, watercolours, and photographs. Although inspired by the woods encircling our house on the lake, "The Green Man" also emerged out of musing upon a fascinating 14th-century carving of a figure who in England these days seems most often to be found on pub signs. I was asked to read it to open the annual Men's Conference held in Kingston, the theme being "Responsibility and The Wild Heart." Cedar Lake also presents itself as Wonderland in "Haley Goes For A Swim," a poem revolving round a young poet's adventures in the underwater world of the imagination, as well as in the subsequent work written in celebration of a landscape that nourishes and sustains my family. Some of the local historical and geographical details energizing "Cedar Lake Rocks" arrive courtesy of friends, neighbours, the Battersea Women's Institute and Doug Bennett's and Tim Tiner's enjoyable guide to the Ontario wilderness, *Up North*. And I fancy I detect a hint of James Reaney's whimsy in the brewing process... The final poem likewise grows out of thanksgiving, this time for the magical Blue Skies Music Festival, an annual event that sprouted up spontaneously 25 years ago as an informal community gathering at Oskar Graf's place in rural Eastern Ontario. I figure about 2000 folks now gather each August in this forested Wonderland for three heat-crazed days of incredible music, holistic workshops, camping and hanging out with old friends. There's even Green Man sightings and timewarps and drums and things that go boom in the night...

THE GREEN MAN

    Green Man
    forest wild
    silent shadow by day,
    moonlight escaping in the whispering
    four-footed dark.
    Hidden face aglow
    sprouting golden rays of leaves
    swirling radiant
    out of 3rd eye
    and the doorway of each plentiful sense
    spiraling down
    to a forgotten sun
    rooted deep
    in storied earth

    Everything that is
    alive and wild
    in the blood
    and scented woods
    peers out of these lustrous almond eyes
    agleam,
    moist with mystery
    brimming with wonder
    and delicate delight,
    eyes that take blossom
    from a bountiful spirit
    ancient as Shield
    sinewy as cedar
    sacred as golden boughs of oak wrapped in mistletoe,
    at home in swamp
    or tree-clad height
    and lost

where you are found

Green-haloed heart
of the antlered forest
torn apart, intact
pulsing across a leafy threshold
centuries-wide
absorbed in vision
beholding a trembling beauty
in deep communion
spellbound
mesmerizing
beckoning . . .

You approach warily
in fear and in awe
reluctant to abandon
your rectangles
and straight lines
of responsibility and duty
the well-trodden cages
of comfort and familiarity
knowing such veils as these
are only parted
by the wild heart
profoundly open
powerfully vulnerable
strong and resilient as red pine
Each step a letting go
a casting off
a deepening longing
to give yourself
over
to total immersion...

It's those eyes
glowing
gently amazed
nurturing and protective
that pull you
deep
into the echoing dappled
domain of moss and fern,
spruce and oak
and the endlessly curving tendrils
of instinct
that ripple up
through the pavement
of your mind

And as you reach out
with that ecstasy you might feel
if a hawk or stag
had come and eaten
out of your palm
something that is
and is not
hand
unfurls out of green air
offering
homecoming

HALEY GOES FOR A SWIM

for Haley, Heather & Walt Freeman

You walk into the lake
as if entering a dream,
a poem
that buoys you up
the deeper you descend
for you allow it
to enter you,
to dream you.
It is assumed
you are half-fish
since of all your family
you remain
immersed
the longest
from 45 seconds
to a year
(for time & space –
those frauds –
curve and bend
like sumac or bamboo
in this world
as much as in outer space
or inner).
Your aunts and uncles,
grandfathers and brothers
you leave on shore
with your shoes
and everyday masks
but here you discover
yourself

one with all
that is
swaying in concert
with water   air   earth   & fire of the sun,
woven into the rippling garment
of cosmos,
something without a name,
closer than breath or thought
lighter than a feather.

And this is what
mermaids know –

how 50 feet below
our dangling feet
and minds
a whole other
realm is in blossom,
a magic forest
where birds are fish
and flowers shells iridescent
with beauty,
a forgotten playground dancing
with forever's children,
a garden no one planted
with colours no one's seen
except the King and Queen
of Elfland
holding court
among the seaweed

– how shores are doors,
looking glasses, rainbows,
phone booths and manhole covers,

wardrobes and stargates,
wishing wells
what have you
and anything can happen
beyond
the hour-glass sands
composing the beach
that slip away
and disappear
like fairies
into the shining web of waves
endlessly nourishing and consuming
one another

– how waves are wings
to fly upon
lifting you lightly
out of yourself
to become something vaster, mysterious,
overflowing into essence

– how to listen
to the wisdom of water:
  Let go . . . let go . . .
you can't hold on
to Neptune, God of Waters,
only fall into his embrace
rise and fall
and flow into rhythms ancient
and primal
the universe dances to
in delight

– how all the treasure chests

escape the clutching hands
of the marketplace
to end up here,
giving forth their gold
and silver
for the free hand of the current
to scatter abundantly
in shimmering arabesques

– how undulating
in a hammock
strung like a rainbow
along the pitch-black floor
of Cedar Lake
looking up
you can see
how our ordinary tick-tock lives
drift by
like the pale bellies
of clouds
the flat unremarkable bottoms
of row boats
until sparkled incandescent
one day
by crystal columns
of light,
golden shafts heaven-born, honey-combed,
wafting like incense
toward the chalice of the heart
in homecoming
here & now
opening the present moment
to Presence . . .

– how to avoid being caught
in nets,
nooses of anchors
and sharp hooks
that puncture wonder
and awe and play,
how to resist
the temptation
of shiny lures
of tin and tinsel
that would wrench you back
into the dry, parched desert of air

– how the bubbles that rise
from this realm
of flux & flow
are called poems,
translucent as pearls
born in depth and silence
of some irritation
the oyster
like a magician
transforms & transmutes
into beauty,
all wounds
being sacred ones,
all worlds
divine,
all words
gifts
arriving on our shore
from theirs,
messages in a bottle
you, mermaid,

Michael Hurley

have been asked
to receive and to read
as your share
of the bounty,
your way
of healing

CEDAR LAKE ROCKS
—*a "homeschooling" poem for Casey & Elena, and visitors to our house*

> "Like the sea, some landforms
> have a metaphysical force . . ."
>
> – Barbara Moon, in *Up North*

> "There are so many rocks in the
> soil north of Kingston that every
> second car is filled with geologists . . ."
>
> – Matt Cohen, in *Ontario*

> "Perspective is everything . . . and nothing."
>
> – Anon.

A Geological Drama:

Scene I

> The rocks underfoot
> or around our backyard campfire
> older than that quicksilver swath
> of stars just out of reach
> overhead
> This ancient land
> stranger than fantasy
> born before heaven . . .

Scene 2

    Sheer age staggers the brain –
    our little house
    barely 10 years old
    still with that "new car smell"
    is perched upon
    the oldest rock in this world
    rock crystallizing harsh and beautiful
    as the fiery new-kid-on-the-block planet
    slowly begins to cool
    its jets in space
    outside human time
    4 billion years ago.

    Welcome to the Amazing

Scene 3

    Fast forward: the soil here
    thin as mist
    over Cedar Lake in the morning
    stretches taut as a drum skin
    over the Canadian Shield
    that vast carapace
    never far beneath our boot heels –
    bedrock breaking through
    the papery skin
    of beleaguered Mother Earth,
    granite outcrops proclaiming us
    knee-deep in ye olde Precambrian basement
    of North America.

Say goodbye to easy farming
and to prim-trim manicured lawns
flashing grass the colour
of the Emerald City

Scene 4

Back up a couple of billion years.
Dear Time-Traveller:
Right where you're standing
this second
was once upon an eon
a fabulous mountain range
high as the Rockies.
Deep in the pit of its churning stomach
molten magma roils and oozes
and shifts uneasily
gets thrown up
then seeps through fissures and cracks
to blend together and harden
as granite
Meanwhile,
a few bewildered bacteria
sole kings of this wild lonely frontier
2 million years back
look on from their single-celled thrones
and shudder

This is the foundation
our house off Battersea Road
and the house called North America
rest upon.
Shield Country.
Cast in stone.

Rock of Ages.

Scene 5

Now blink –
Time sweeps the unseen
mountain giants away
into the dustbin of prehistory
but can't quite whittle away
these industrial-strength weather-resistant
hard-as-nails granite domes
like the ones our canoe scrapes along
as we land on the shore
of Cedar Lake
to visit neighbours
here in Freeman Territory

Blink again
a couple of times
each one a million years
and the scene changes
like a kaleidoscope –
vast tropical seas
surround and submerge us.
Watch out for that whale!
Attention: incoming sharks
the size of runways
have the right of way.
And all these mammoth and microscopic
carcasses pile up
on the soup-warm sea bottom
tastefully garnished with the decaying plants
of endless underwater jungles

Welcome to Immensity

Untold sediment of marine life
writing itself
into limestone
Enough raw material
to build Canada's first capital
Kingston
82 million times
with what's left over
recrystallizing
to become marble
magical mystical stone canvass
upon which native peoples nearby
will paint petroglyph visions
of the 82 million realities.
Rock of Sages.
600 million years ago
it's all seascape
The real estate market is slow:
no life on dry land
to speak of.
If you look closely
you might spot
the first multicellular organisms
out for a swim
and later . . . a crawl
A blazing meteorite
hurtling overhead
makes you blink again
as it smashes into
"Algonquin Park"
(no one was hurt)
leaving a hole

>you can still see
>450 million years later
>And some 50 million years
>after this light show
>what's that underfoot?
>Let's call it
>the world's first soil.
>Dandelions are not far off.
>Or dinos.

Scene 6 or 7 or whatever

>Wave after wave
>of glaciers –
>nature's sandpaper –
>give the entire continent
>the cold shoulder.
>White bulldozers 4 km. thick
>rolling up and down the countryside
>a gigantic ploughing match
>scraping away at the soft belly
>of sediment
>scouring it down
>to barebones Shield
>once again.
>This walking ice storm
>chews up the turf
>for 100,000 years

>Welcome to the Monstrous

>One long blink
>brings you 10,000 years ago –
>almost home.

The humongous Champlain Sea
has just retreated
(thankyouverymuch).
Lake Algonquin
on a Great Lakes scale
(and thus a post-glacial pipsqueak)
fills in for it.
Good riddance to the last glacier
(a fair weather friend in reverse)
hightailing it past James Bay
to the Arctic
delivering one final (final?)
pummelling to the place
and (messy as an uninvited bear
at your campsite)
leaving the front yard strewn
with boulders and debris and whatnot
plus all that gravel
for the Roads Dept.
meanwhile making off with as much soil
as it can get its size 1000 paws on
Our neighbours
a few desperate farmers
poking about in this thinness
that's only had 10 short millennia
to amount to something
since the last hit-and-run deep-freeze
pirated the good earth away
God knows where
can be seen out proddin' and cajoling
the stony unforgiving land
knowing all too well
that the Shield
don't erode much

this far north
that it's a goddamn miser
in fact
bent on hoarding
every last microscopic mineral particle
with only a precious few wrestled away
by erosion and weather
and other double-edged swords

A small womb, indeed
though not barren
and fruitful in her way
if fragile:
my son falls playing soccer
his knee scraping rock
older than the Big Dipper,
an eight-year old erasing thousands of years' worth
of hard work
in a painful split second
as worlds collide.
Every now and then
somebody ploughs up the prehistoric –
cuz look what the cat
(a sabre-tooth)
brought in after the glacier:
woody mammoths & mastodons
lugging their skyscraper skeletons about
all those bones rattling about
beneath your John Deere
or your minivan
and – get this –
giant beavers
(as if the regular ones
aren't trouble enough)

weighing in at 200 kg
(440 lbs., Dad).
That's one hell of a BIG dam.

Welcome to the Bizarre

Blink: a birch-bark canoe
(another aboriginal invention)
glides by
7000 years ago
on Cedar Lake
hugging the shoreline
where long ago
a herd of thirsty cedars
comes by to browse
for the night
and ends up staying centuries.
Leaving their footprints
in the sunset sky
and along the standing-room-only shore
a light green necklace
draped round a lake everchanging
in texture, colour and mood
they leave too a name
bearing a royal ancestry:
the King of France
christens you *arbor vitae*
"The Tree of Life"
"The Wonder Tree"
whose healing tea brewed by native peoples
(who hold you sacred)
saves Jacques Cartier
and his scurvy crew
that first unreal winter of 1536

in a world
new to them
and strange and frightening
beyond belief

Scene 2300

Three more superblinks
and as many clicks of your heels:
You are entering
ROCKLAND
the original name
I love so much
given this small wilderness settlement of
"Ansley's Mills"
that soon becomes
"VanLuven's Mills"
(after a U.E.L. Lundy's Lane vet & patriarch)
that later becomes
in the Storrington Township Council minutes 1857
Battersea
(namesake of the English birthplace
of my grandmother).
ROCKLAND
on the rough & tumble
"Old Stage Route"
14 forever miles north of
Fort Frontenac/Kingston
formerly *Kataraqui* –
"the place where the land and the rocks
rise out of the waters
at the end of the lake
of shining waters"
aka "The Garden of the Gods"

to the Iroquois
the great Onondaga Oneida & Mohawk
greeting Count Frontenac in July 1673
(who within a week
builds walls around the garden) . . .

ROCKLAND
Rock garden:
"great outcroppings
of bald-faced granite
appeared among the well-timbered land"
suitable for erecting churches upon
unsuitable for most anything else
(besides beauty
if you've the temperament)
like nixing a sewage system
or community water works
for starters.
And RIGHT HERE
(X marks the spot)
"south of the village
the out-crop of rock changes
from the familiar limestone
to pre-Cambrian granite."
Which is basically
pre-anything, eh.
And in Temperance-be-damned Granite House
Battersea's first tavern
(great great granddaddy of The Creek)
the 5cents-a-glass whiskey
washes down news of gristmills,
log jams, fishin' & huntin' hot spots, tall tales,
the price of wheat, falling tree accidents,
house fires, shivarees, new preachers,

and the miraculous construction of the CPR –
15000 men immortalizing 1884
by blowing other ageless Shield rocks
byjeezus right back to the stars
their younger siblings
while 3 this-side-up dynamite factories
going at it night & day
push the blasted railway
across godforsaken blackfly territory
(*"I'll die with the blackflies
a-pickin' my bones"*).
Plus 4000 sweatin' horses
and 300 yelping dogsleds
pulling Progress & Prosperity
Prudence & Propriety
and a watch-your-language parlour
full of other gods
right into your living room.

Welcome to Queen Victoria's colony.

And then
in the blink of a 3rd eye
or less
in the fraction of a fraction
of a nanosecond
(divided by 100)
maybe just to balance things out
or stir 'em up
Nancy & Michael, Casey & Elena
beam down into ROCKLAND
rolling the rocks
back into the fields
and the imagination

the farmers and forest-fighters cleared,
planting and hugging new trees
and going out back
for a canoe ride or swim
where once upon a timewarp
a 1500-story high block of ice
melted in a 1/2 mile pockmark
Old Man Glacier obligingly gouged out
or maybe
(if local lore be believed)
a stray meteorite
playing hookey from the Perseids perhaps
dug in its shiny heels
50 to 70 to who knows how many
giant steps deep
into the heart of ROCKLAND
and deeper still
into childhood memories
and the idle musings
of rockhounds and historians
geologists and poets
and other lucky stargazers –
and, of course,
folks just like you
who find their way
somehow or other
right here
right now

P.S. Don't blink.

NOBODY LEAVES HERE: MUSINGS UPON THE BST (BLUE SKIES TIMEWARP)

"Perhaps I took part in the first dozen or so Blue Skies Music Festivals, but in a sense I only went to one."

– Greg Forbes, *Nothing But Blue Skies*

"Blue Skies is magic."

– Paul Gervan, *Nothing But Blue Skies*

"I just sit back and let it happen."

– Oskar Graf, *Nothing But Blue Skies*

No matter how many times
you've come & gone
once you're here
and the good ol' Blue Skies earth music
rises up to greet you
somehow
it's as if
you've never left.
It's kind of a feeling . . .
You're walking about in the meadow
caressed by the whole scene
and suddenly a frisbee
sails into your hand
like a smoke-ring
circling forever
and it's the same one
you just threw
3 years back

Or you turn round
to find a familiar face
emerging from a tent
or the Magoo Loo,
maybe crystallizing out of a food line
or a cascading circle
of ecstatic square dancers
and you casually pick up
in mid-sentence
a conversation left hovering
like a musical note
some 12 moons ago.

Except the "ago" and the "back when"
seem kinda unreal
faded somehow
the time in between –
those other 360 odd evanescent days –
a grey flicker
like frames in a grainy old
black & white film
cuz – WHOOSH! SHAZAM!! –
now you're up and over
the rainbow
and colour streams into your life
like Canada geese in spring
shining forth from blue skies
sparkling like so many candles
on a gigantic birthday cake
celebrating everybody
And the sour turns sweet
and the turmoil seems ordained
as we're gathered into this moment
in all its synchronistic glory

and decades-spanning choreography
and it's kind of a feeling
like you're inside the Horn of Plenty
and each festival brings
another ritual circling of the spiral
winding us deeper
into some timeless core of ourselves,
wrapping us round & round
one another
and every fun-lovin' blade
of Blue Skies grass,
amp-ing up the Magic
'til like a spinning top
thru the mellow mayhem
you can hear it hum
from out of a motionless quiet centre
HERE WE ALL ARE
RIGHT HERE AND NOW

And even in the obligatory downpour
and the muddy midst
of cheek-by-jowl tents
it sets your heart dancing
and your spirit flying
deeper into the festive rhythms
of this country garden of delights,
wildflower rhythms
you want to imagine
your whole life moving in concert with,
like babies swimming in bellies or hawks riding thermals
and strolling along the hilltop
overlooking the main stage
you stop to wonder
at the shape 2000 lives make

for themselves
by making do
with the moment
as it is,
letting go
into the windborne currents
of an endless present,
foregoing for 3 days
fantasies that the future's
something you decide about
and order around
like a cadet on parade square . . .

Just sitting back
into this spacious time-out moment
letting chaos & harmony
unfold as they see fit,
coalescing and diverging
& drifting effortlessly together again
with family and friends
and a field full of folks
all floating through this sky blue day
like those feathery skip-to-my-Lou milkweed seeds
kids instinctively release
from their tight little pods.
And you remember carting in your stuff
fastening your tent stakes
and looking up to find
your sons & your daughters
already given over
to the festival's flux & flow,
already following the Pied Piper's magic flute
thru holes in parental walls
into Never - Never Land.

They are colourful tie-dyed kites now
escaping far beyond
your back-home reasons and rules
your tidy illusions
of who-makes-the-decisions-round-here
and you gently let go
their straining strings
to see them sailing out of sight
headlong into their own waiting lives
unchaperoned unsunscreened unprepared unperturbed
just wanting to get on with it.

So you fish about in the cooler
for something to munch on
or take later to Gord & Barb's tent
but the Blue Skies Magic
wants *you* as well
& it somehow takes to rolling back
the age-ometer
until you feel that freedom child
stirring like longing
inside you too,
cracking thru the cocoon
of non-stop split-second scheduling
and frantic deadlining,
urging you deeper into the slipstream
of your own mystery
spread out before you now
like a feast you get up from
and return to
but never really exit
And suddenly you remember
Greg reminiscing about Blue Skies
bent over a guitar

in his basement studio, saying
"Once on the site
I always had the impression
I'd never left..."

Blue Skies is funny that way.
It's kind of a feeling...
Must have something to do
with that there Gatehouse
– somethin' 'bout coming upon
that barnboard Brigadoon place
at the end of a dusty droney highway journey
just sitting in the trees there
with folks arriving
like rays of sunshine
escaping from behind a cloud
to light up
this unlikely feast
hidden deep in the forest...
light from that part of the spectrum
that's invisible as dreams or buried gold
the rest of the year...
And passing thru them gates
it's like crossing over
some enchanted threshold
slipping through the looking glass
wardrobe phonebooth manhole cover
secret door stargate
whatever
into... the mystic

Not unlike those resonant Haida Gwaii myths
about borderworlds:
forestedge   seasurface   blueskydome

– once your hook disappears
under those waters
who knows what it'll reel in
the strangest thing always being
common magic
as Bronwen calls it
the ordinary revealing itself as extraordinary
the unusual flip-flopping over into the everyday
– y' know,
the reg'lar otherworld flora & fauna
3 daysnights of Blue Skies
gently immerses you in
as you tuck the planets to bed
to the strains of Night Sun
or Reverend Ken and His Lost Followers.
It's kind of a feeling
like the ones kids get
hanging upside down
or walking backwards
and some say it wafts out of the woods
cradling the Tipi
to blanket Oskar's whole patch of land
and you could miss it
cuz it's everywhere.
In the tent across from you
someone is casually pulling on their pants
as if they're at home
and they are, really
and so are you
for that matter
as you brush away at your teeth
in a sea of passersby
or idly pick someone else's towel
off a branch

to wash whatever sleep you got
from your timetrippy eyes
the better to see the day
ripen slow & full & juicy
as a prize watermelon
fattening itself on the lazy summer heat
and spilling out of this country cornucopia

Sure, some things seem to tumble
out of the timewarp
a tad different –
that little pony-tail girl
in the blue cotton dress
sifting sand thru slow-motion hands
down in the Kids' Area
is a young woman with wings now
and your son
("You have kids!?")
who wouldn't be caught dead
in her general vicinity
can't quite seem
to escape her barefoot bangled orbit
today
as she and a pod of other
beautifully alien adolescent life-forms
set the hillside aflame
with their halcyon dancing
And a touch of grey
leaching out from Kingston limestone
appears to have travelled
thru the atmosphere
to settle upon the remaining hair
gracing you and your peers
at this peerless musical picnic

But that's just small potatoes –
the Groove's still fresh & clear & strong
cuz as you can see
there's the same late-night-all-night folks
still boogieing away to God's music
like they just got religion
& aren't sure whether their souls
are leaving their bodies
or finally entering them
but hey, either way,
it sure feels good, Lord
as the moon bodysurfs on upraised arms
lifting it higher into the serenaded heavens.
And look! –
here's Jeff & Linda, Sue & Chris, and
there's John the Farmer
not seen in these parts
since – GOSH! – '75 or '76
and byjaysus here he is
a'drummin' away
as though he's never missed a beat
and he and that dayglo kite overhead
and the sultry afternoon and the smell of roast corn
and the wild meltdown dancing and the smiles on the faces
and the ragamuffin kids and the sacred feelgood vibes
the choir the carts the camping gear
Robbie the Magician & the storytelling circle
the stage announcements and the incense of wood smoke
– all are weaving threads & songlines
that connect
our life
our great big small beautiful communal individual Blue Skies
Life

in a funkydoodle serendipitous Blue Skies Dreamtime
Tapestry.
Yeah!

It's kind of a feeling . . .
a Campfire Zen Physics feeling
for the more we weave it together
the more it unravels time & space
– those clever frauds –
so they curve and bend
like sumac or bamboo
in Blue Skies
as much as in outerspace
or inner
And folks given half a chance
tend to turn inside-out here
so the odds are greater
rounding a bend in Sleepy Hollow, say,
of entering each other's dreams
and visions and born-in quirkiness
and crazy beauty and footloose deepdown selves
that are just gonna shine thru anyway
whether the hands on the clock
read 1974 or 2001

Or something like that.
Theories abound.
*("Huge spiritually-magnetic you know ley lines
like at Egypt or Stonehenge
criss-cross like spaghetti
in the Precambrian Shield here
4-1/2 inches beneath our Birkenstocks,
see, and like they emanate these . . .")*

86 Michael Hurley

Yeahwhudever.
It's kind of a feeling . . .

I guess it isn't exactly
that time stops at Blue Skies
but that it doesn't stop
dancing its brains out
dancing and dipping and diving
deep into the eternal now,
revelling in the gift of the Present.
Maybe all that luminous music
shimmering in the air,
bubbling up out of the ground
raining down from above
and rising up from the firepits
has just got Old Father Time
as giddy as
a whirling dervish Sufi clown
so hurdy gurdy high on the still point
of the toss & turning world
he keeps on grinning and spinning out and about
the same wonderful site
the same lonnnnggggg weekend
the same warm folks (but more so)
same friendly faces & goodtime gathering of the tribes
the same but different river . . .

Welcome home,
friend,
to what is
still
the first
Blue Skies Music Festival

LORNE SHIRINIAN

LORNE SHIRINIAN

fled toronto before the flood rose higher than a kite. i held my breath all the way to the border. found a key under the mat. set up house. then the gates opened. and it was a milky exodus. but I've always gone the other way. dowsed my fateful and bumped up hard against leviticus. certifcates of authenticity. 101 ways to skin a cat any way you cut it.

i stayed there far too many. stasis too long. minds like a sack of st. lawrence cement. then clipped wings were given the royal nudge and off i went my lost years to recover. the valley just wasn't deep enough but oh, the craggy walls were imposing.

and that's how i arrived. metropolis noir. halfway city of the eternal circle. offering possibilities of triangulation 'cause i need to know where i am. and there's just enough horizon for me to get a relative bearing. and so i often take my pulse. check mirrors. here are the vital signs:

born:	toronto
some letters:	Honours BA in French Lang & Lit, U of T, MA in Comparative Lit, Carleton, PhD in Comparative Lit, Université, de Montréal
some mistakes:	far too many
some job:	head, dept. of english, royal military college of canada
some books:	4 collections of poetry, 3 collections of stories, 5 scholarly monographs, a few film scripts, (2 novels in a drawer)
my life:	noémi, emmanuel & benjamin
my hopes:	our boys, more poems, stories, novels, and films reel soon

The stories that follow are from a new collection of stories I'm preparing titled *Memory's Orphans*. The poems, 'Labyrinth," "Headlong Fall," and "The Door Ajar," are from my new collection, *Rough Landing*.

HIDE AND SEEK

He never liked it when friends of his parents came for a visit. They always made a fuss over him by calling him all kinds of sweet names and endearments in Armenian and by patting his head and pinching his cheeks. He always found this embarrassing because he didn't know how to act or what to say. When everyone's attention turned away, he would steal off and hide in the Don Valley until they left. It's not that he was a wild child. Truthfully, he was fascinated by these people who were so familiar yet so strange at the same time. The throaty Armenian language they spoke together was warm and comforting to him in a way that English never could be, yet more and more, English invaded his thoughts until he had to force himself to understand his parents' language. Not too long ago, he began to speak English at home. His parents spoke to him only in Armenian, but he obstinately refused to respond in their language. English was so much easier, more natural as it seemed linked to the world around him. Armenian tasted of pilaf and spiced lamb, Armenian pizzas called *lahmajoon*, *madzoon*-yogurt, mint, garlic and onions, eggplant, okra, green beans and tomato. It was home. But it was also the language of whisperings. Often when his parents' friends came over and drank tea or dark coffee in delicate demi-tasse cups and ate Armenian cookies and pastries, he would hear them from above on the stairs on which he sat quietly observing. They used words he didn't understand until one day he asked his father, who told him, Not yet; I'll tell you soon enough. You're not ready yet. One time he heard the word, *tchart*, and understood it meant massacre. From the stairs, he sat above and listened to Armenians recount what had happened to them all in 1915. Mrs. Voski told of how her husband had been killed and she had to carry her children as she was forced across the Syrian desert. Albert became a teary-eyed, five-year old boy again as he described how the Turkish soldiers cut his father in two and ripped open his sister's stomach. My father and mother whispered back and forth as tears filled their eyes. Their friends shook their heads in disbelief, knowing all too well the truth of the horror; others nodded in sympathy for their great pain. And always the whisperings.

Once, the young boy decided to make a point of coming down the stairs. He quietly worked his way to the door of the living room and stood at the threshold. Suddenly, the whispering stopped. His mother dried her eyes and held her arms out to her son, whom she held and kissed. Mrs. Kasparian poured him some mint tea and placed a cookie on a plate for him. Then men began talking about business, and the women discussed recipes and community news. He looked intently into their eyes and saw that the pain contained in the whispers was still there. He turned and ran out of the house and down into the valley where he lay on the grassy slope and watched the puffy clouds overhead. He mouthed the words, *Armenia, Hayastan, Armenia*, and watched the wind blow the clouds into different formations.

One Sunday afternoon, some new people came to the house. He watched them from his parents' bedroom window at the front of the house. There was something new this time; these people had a young girl his age. He watched for too long and realized that he had missed his chance of escape. He had no choice now but to go down and meet these people as his father called his name.

Krikor and Maral, this is our son James.

They patted his head and cheeks and called him sweet names in Armenian. Then the father guided his daughter forward.

James, this is Anahid.

She greeted him in Armenian, and he responded, Nice to meet you, in English.

He knew what was coming. His father suggested that they go off and play together.

Don't go too far, his father said. Come back in a while for some tea and pastries. And don't get dirty!

Come on, he told Anahid. Let's go, and he ran off across the street to the valley, but when he looked back Anahid was standing still, uncertain of what to do. Come on; it's okay. We'll play. Maybe she doesn't understand English, he thought. He went back to her and told her in Armenian that he was going to show her his favourite hiding spot in the valley. He took her hand and coaxed her to follow.

They worked their way down the slippery slope, holding on to thin trees and green leafy bushes. Part way down, he showed her a path that took them to a cliff face where he had hollowed out a little cave that overlooked the Don River. They nestled in side by side and looked out at the valley.

Where are you from? he asked.

Alexandria.

Where's that?

Egypt.

How long have you been in Canada?

Not long. Maybe six months.

Suddenly, they heard the snapping of twigs and footsteps through the brush from the path above them. He put his right forefinger to his lips, Shshsh, and pulled her back into the hollow so that they would not be seen.

Is it a Turk? the girl asked.

The boy was puzzled by this question. What would Turks be doing here? He told her it was probably some of the boys who lived down the street and that it would be better that they didn't find them. He didn't want anyone to know about his hiding spot.

They sat quietly for some time watching the birds circling overhead and listening for footsteps.

Do you want to play a game? Anahid asked.

Sure. What do you want to play? James asked.

What we're doing now, she said. Let's pretend the Turks have come to our village and have taken our fathers and brothers away and that all the children and women are being gathered into a column to be marched out of town.

James wondered at such a strange game, yet there was an uncomfortable familiarity about it he couldn't name.

What shall we do? he asked.

Well, we have run away to safety. Everyone is going to be killed, and we are hiding. They mustn't find us, or they will do terrible things to us.

Anahid's eyes filled with tears. James wondered what kind of game this was that made her cry.

They mustn't find us. We'll protect each other, won't we?

Of course, James told her. I'll protect you.

He cleaned his hand on his chest and brushed the tears from her eyes and pulled back her dark hair. He patted her cheek, Don't worry, he told her.

She leaned her head on his shoulder, and he breathed her in. He was embarrassed by this familiarity. This young Armenian girl from another world was so strange to him. But she had begun to awaken in him things he wasn't sure of, things he may have heard whispered. Sounds like images. Sounds like tears in his mother's eyes. Sounds of columns pushed east. Metallic sounds of bayonets and scimitars. The smell of blood whispered. Things he could only imagine darkly as she leaned her head against his.

We have to eat to stay alive, he told her. The only thing I have is a stick of Juicy Fruit. He pulled it from the yellow paper wrapper then opened the silver cover and folded the gum in half and tore it in two. Here. This will do us for a while; then, we'll have to find other food.

I can bake bread, she told him. Can you find some wheat?

I'll go out at night and get some. And water too. I'll make a fire.

Won't the Turks see it? she asked.

Yes, you're right. I'll get a blanket then.

Yes, a blanket will be good, she said.

Again they heard the footsteps and whoops of noise and laughter from the boys who lived down the street, returning along the path above them. Anahid and James leaned against each other. She held her hand over her mouth and pressed herself hard and trembled against James. When things became quiet again, she said, The Turks have gone for now. But they'll come back. They always come back.

Far in the distance from the street, they heard James' father calling them.

We'd better go, he said.

They climbed hand-in-hand back up the cliff face, then along the path and up the grassy slope, holding on to trees and bushes until they reached the top.

There you are, you monkey, his father said. Where were you?

He asked Anahid if she was all right, and they all went into the house to wash up and have some tea. His mother poured everyone a cup of mint tea and passed around a tray of sweets.

Where did you go? Anahid's mother asked.

We played hide and seek in the valley, she told her.

But there were only two of you. How did you play?
We played it the Armenian way, she told her.

Her mother smiled and laughed, not quite sure of what her daughter meant. The conversation quickly continued as before. Anahid sat across from James and sipped her tea. She looked over the rim of the cup into his eyes and smiled.

Slowly, he began to hear things. He placed his cup back onto the saucer with a fragile ring. Throaty syllables filled his mind...he saw *tchart*, the massacres, made tangible as the language invaded his thoughts.

Everyone was whispering.

Everyone all around was whispering.

He opened his mouth and tried to speak, but no matter how hard he tried, he could only whisper.

A sound and an image, a small, bright ray of light shone inside him.

And he added his voice to that of his family.

EXTRAS

(Members of the cast who speak no lines and make no gestures but are used primarily as part of the background or as part of a crowd.)

1

My name is Art Marginalian. I'm an actor. You may have seen me on screen; I've appeared in a lot of productions. I'm usually in the front line of a crowd behind the action, or I'll walk imperceptibly by the talent in the foreground. Just a guy on the street off somewhere. Most of you wouldn't even care; you're focused elsewhere on the big screen. Sometimes, I'll look off frame as I move effortlessly past the camera. I won't do anything to detract from the main action of the shot; I am a professional and take my work seriously, but I will try to do something to make my moment credible and interesting for the little time I'm on. I'm an extra. No one really notices me. That means I've done my work well.

On set, I do my thing for as many takes necessary until the director is satisfied. Between the scenes in which I am supposed to appear, I hang around well back so as not to interfere with the crew setting up, but I can't be too far away in case I'm called. Usually, I will be reading or eating some nuts and raisins to keep my energy level up when the third assistant director will suddenly come puffing over in a hurry, his brow all sweaty, "Come on; let's go. We need you on set now!" And all the extras will be herded over to their spots while the director frames the shot. Over the years I've been lucky. I work steadily and often. There's been lots of work in

Toronto over the past years, especially with American productions coming here because of our cheap dollar. And casting knows I'm a trusted commodity, as they say. I won't screw up. I'll give what is needed every time. Tell me where to move and how, and I'll do it. You want fake background talking, yelling, or moaning, even a pratfall, I can deliver. I can cry on cue. I love doing this; it seems to come naturally to me. And I can strike out violently in a second. Whatever is called for. I do what is required then go home.

I love my life. I get to observe human nature closely every day. I get to adopt different personae even if I'm well in the background or part of a large crowd. I need a reason for being where I am. This is the real challenge. For example, last week I was seated at a table with three fellow office workers, Lynn, the Asian girl, Jessica, the fair Anglo-Saxon, and Marcia, the African-American, in a scene we did together for Holman Radley, who's making the picture for Bi-Mark. The working title is *Tunnel Vision*. Here's the scene: the four of us are computer programmers for NewCon, a hi-tech conglomerate in Atlanta. About ten of us are at lunch when three terrorists break in and hold us hostage. Suddenly and very violently, all at our table are blown away with shotgun blasts, but we do have a nice moment in which we are having coffee not too far away from the hero and heroine, Lawson Mighty and Alna Nastrovia, who become the principal hostages. The four of us are talking about implementing the new high-band width connection software we've been working on for over a year and joking, but not too overtly, when the terrorists break in. You know, for a few seconds, I believe I was on to solving one of the major problems we had been having with the computer code. I think I captured this in a certain facial expression I found. To no avail, however. To show they are mean and very serious, the terrorists shoot everyone at our table. That was lots of fun. We all had to be reset with squib packs of explosives and blood for four takes until our deaths looked right. The director had me shot first. I went down arms flailing; then Lynn was killed. She's pushed back by the blast and ends up falling face down over me. The fun part was that we had to hold our positions while they checked the monitors. Then when they liked the shot, they had to set up for the next sequence with us still highly visible in the frame. So we had to keep very still. Lynn kept on tickling my left nipple ever so slightly with her forefinger the whole time we were down. I thought I was going to lose it. But we are very professional, and the scene, I'm told, looks authentic and quite frightening.

Since we were killed off, that was all for us in that production, although I was called back for a shot in which the terrorists round up a roomful of programmers and lock them in a closet. I got to wear a blonde wig and beard for this scene. I made sure I was barely visible behind the other programmers just in case I could be recognized. No fear of that though.

That was last week. I've worked three days this week and now have two days off before my next shoot. By the sounds of it, this next project is something big. Maria Bevalacqua, my agent, got me eight successive days of work with the possibility of several other full days later on. But now, I've got two days to do nothing but sleep and read and meet friends at our favourite café on Queen West. I'm really looking forward to this next job. I wonder who I'll be and what my situation is. It won't matter to the director as long as I bring it off before the camera. I love reinventing myself. I love being an extra.

2

Early one chilly November morning in Toronto not long after my arrival from Kingston, I received a call from Maria Bevalacqua of the Screen Extras Guild, calling about a job. Just in time, too. My stay with Hovaness was wearing a little thin. He was getting quite serious about his new girlfriend, and I was obviously in the way. Still, he let me crash for as long as I needed. I fumbled for the phone and barely got hello out.

"Hey, are you awake?"

"Yeah, I am. I'm up."

"You sure? Good. Listen. I've got something for you. Allan Carmichael is shooting a film for United up here. They're going to be doing some scenes at the Yorkdale Mall for about a week; there's work for you for five days. Crowd stuff, you know. Also, I've got you in the background behind some pretty intense stuff between Gina Hershel and Rob Lukas in a restaurant. Yeah, you're with your date or whatever, eating at a table. It's good exposure. Hello? Say thank you."

"Ave Maria. Thank you."

"You're welcome. The contact person is Meryl Blossom. Break a leg. Bye. Wait! How long you gonna be around? Good. I'll see what else I can find for you. Keep in touch."

Work for five days. Enough for some food, a few books and a ticket out. Perfect.

The next morning despite my protests, Hovaness drove me up to Yorkdale off the 401 and stopped near Sears where we went through our little ritual:

Me: Thanks for letting me stay. I hope things work ourt for you and Verjiné,.

Hovaness: Yeah, thanks. She's special, isn't she? Keep in touch. See you the next time through.

I pulled open the glass door and left the outside world and entered the mall world to find that the crew had appropriated one hallway of the huge shopping expanse for the shoot. I checked it out then crossed over from the mall world onto the transformed mall set and looked for Meryl Blossom. People brushed by me before I could get a syllable out. Finally, someone slowed down long enough to point vaguely off in one direction, "Over there, I think." I walked over to a small crowd of people engaged in an intense discussion.

"Excuse me, I'm looking for Meryl Blossom."

"I'm Meryl. Who wants to know?"

"I'm Emmanuel Levy-Torossian. I'm playing Todd."

"Ah, you're here then. Good."

She scribbled something onto a sheet and ripped it off the pad.

"Here. Take this over to wardrobe and make-up to see what they can do."

Wardrobe didn't like my shirt. The pattern and colours would be too distracting in the background. People would focus on me rather than on the action in the foreground. They found a drab beige one and matched it with a solid, dark brown tie.

"Here try these. This will help you disappear."

I turned and tucked the shirt in my pants then turned and looked in the mirror. "Yeah, that's it,' she said. "The shoes are a little scuffed, but they won't show up in the frame. And lose the coat, okay. Just the shirt and tie. The pants aren't great, but they won't show up either."

The wardrobe person then directed me over to make-up where I was commanded to sit. A young girl with tousled blond hair came over, carrying a large case and checked my sheet.

"Hi, I'm Sherry." She started working on my face.

"So, Todd, you're in the scene behind Ron and Gina. Great. I'm just going to put a little pancake on to cut the glare. Do you always wear your hair that way?"

I told her I normally did but that she could change it as she liked.

"I don't have much time, but maybe if I pulled it back like this. It'll change your personality too. Make you more of a Todd. Wadyathink?"

The third AD, assistant director, came over and called everyone in the shot to take their places on the set. The set dresser was doing a final round. Cups of real coffee were poured and were appropriately steaming. Half-eaten croissants were placed at the right angle on the plates. I was told to sit at the table one row removed from the action, still very close to the camera though. My date welcomed me with a handshake.

"Hi, I'm Lorna Weinstein. I'm playing Caroline."

"Hi, nice to meet you," I said.

While Allan Carmichael was looking through the lens to set everything he wanted into the frame, we discussed how we would play our parts.

"Do you want to be lovers having a meal together?" she asked. "Or should this be our first date, and we're feeling each other out? Or should we be a very married couple resting after a day's shopping?"

"Not bad," I told her. "We could have just met. I mean I spotted you sitting alone, was attracted and took my chance by coming over. You invited me to sit, and we're feeling each other out."

"Yeah, that's good too."

Before we had a chance to make a final decision, the principal actors came on the set and took their places. Now the serious framing began. Allan asked me to move six inches left so as not to obtrude against Rob's profile. Lorna had to move six inches right, and there we were, very close when Allan spoke out, "Okay everybody, we're going to do a series of establishing shots from different angles. Hold your positions when I say cut. Okay?"

Then they went through the routine as we focused: "Lights. Sound. Speed. Camera rolling...And action... Cut. How's the gate? The gate's clean. Sound? Sound's clean."

"Okay print it. Let's set up over here. Actors, hold your positions. After this one, we'll take three minutes of ambient sound."

While Lorna and I stared intently at each other, the principals had some make-up retouched.

We spent the whole morning doing this, never having a chance to really speak. We broke for lunch. Lorna went shopping. I went to a W. H. Smith bookstore and bought a David Goodis novel, *Shoot the Piano Player*, a 1990 reprint from Black Lizard Press, and then sat in a café a few stores down from the set until I heard the call for the afternoon's shoot.

We took our places again. This was to be the big scene. They wanted to film it early while the energy levels were still high. Allan huddled with Gina and Rob and went over where they were emotionally.

"Don't worry, kids," he told them, "you can't go over the top on this. We'll do as many takes as we need to cover ourselves to get it right."

Allan had us acting with the cameras and sound rolling for about two minutes before he yelled action. My solid, dark brown tie was properly adjusted. Sherry had gone over my face and hair. I was ready. Lorna looked great with her long dark hair brushed straight down over her shoulders. She had beautiful dark eyes which she used effectively to motivate me during our scene.

For those two minutes, we just stared into each other's eyes longingly and savoured our coffee. We spoke softly about whatever came into our minds, surrounded by the afternoon crowd at the mall.

Action!

The principals began. I wanted to look over but managed to maintain some degree of professionalism. While Lorna and I feigned love, Gina and Rob started into each other.

Gina: You're an egotistical bastard. The only person you care about is you. You aren't capable of love.

Rob: That's good coming from you. What've you ever given me that I didn't have to take or beg for?

Gina: Perhaps if you were around more, you wouldn't have to beg.

Rob: What's that supposed to mean?

Gina: Perfect. You don't know, do you? You're never here, Rob. Half the time I don't know where you are.

Rob jumped up and kicked his chair back; we all turned around shocked.

Rob: Yeah, well, you won't have to worry about where I am again.

Rob stormed out of the frame.

"Cut! That was great. Let's do it again. This time I want you to try this."

The three went into a huddle again. We had our cups refilled and our faces touched up. Rob and Gina took their places and went at it again six more times until Allan was satisfied. Then he covered himself with shot/reverse shot stuff and the major mall scene for the day was over.

Lorna offered me a ride back into the city. She lived on the other side of Spadina Road west of Forest Hill but asked me to put myself into her hands and took me to a café she liked on the Danforth. Although the room was full, we managed to the get a seat in the window and spent three hours exploring ideas and futures while people on the sidewalk outside passed us by. I wasn't used to being so close like that, being framed and exposed. It made me feel uncomfortable.

On the final day of shooting at the mall, Frederick, the first AD, wanted the extras who were in the café scene to be shot walking past Gina and Rob, who were now making up on one of the broad alleyways of the mall. We set up. Lorna was handed a green shopping bag from Halton's, stuffed full of paper, I was given a plastic bag from The Scribe bookstore with two blank books in it.

"You two walk arm in arm. You're in love, and you've just spent a beautiful afternoon shopping at the mall and having coffee together. You were in the background; the audience will remember you from the café. They saw your reaction to each other. Just maintain it. Okay, let's try it."

On action, we strolled through the frame well behind Rob and Gina who had made up and were now kissing.

Cut!

We did this for at least thirty minutes until Allan was happy with the shot. On the wrap, I handed in my bag, shirt and tie and said good-bye to Lorna, who was meeting friends in the west end. I made my hair recognizable again then put on my jacket and walked through the mall to the subway station.

On the underground ride back into the city, I wondered what the film was about. I only saw my small bit in it and really couldn't see how all the parts we did fit together, whether or not they made sense. But then that's the good thing about being an extra. Whatever happens, you don't react unnecessarily. The principal action takes place well away from you, while you act out your very minor part in the background. It may appear unimportant, yet somehow, what you do makes it all seem real.

LABYRINTH

it begins this way:
a hairline so fine
barely visible but
certainly there
in ordinary light

then faint tributaries
tiny branches
tubes of weak blood
mark a new irrigation system
in your head

deep one night in anxious sleep
a full river etches its course and canyons
through our unsuspecting thoughts
you open your eyes under a startled full moon
and try to dam the raging flow
but the surge balloons
and soon there's a crack
elastic tissue is breached
and the dark lines trace the fearful labyrinth

and there
a series of random lines
made real in the fragile skull
connect and disappear
the minotaur is loosed
its dark secret set free
you put your hand out
feel for walls
and take measured steps

HEADLONG FALL
(in which i prove the theory)

the slope
    or incline
        accelerates inclination

i discovered this
    during our conversation
        in the smile you spoke
            and now my brakes are shot
                but at this velocity they're of no use

and now i'm fighting for control
    in my headlong fall
        as if i'd taken an unsuspecting
                      step
                          beyond
the age
    and edge
        of some steep thought

and if in my swift descent
    desire makes me bold
        and before my fateful landing
            i place my hand upon your thigh
                i wonder what i will do if you sigh

THE DOOR AJAR

the door opens a crack
                dropping
a thin line of light across the floor
an invitation and a dare

the door and its mystery
plant hard desire
incite a flaccid step
harsh seduction at the threshold
of an aging thought

the slit widens
confirms a dark premonition
nowhere to hide
in the blinding clarity

no shadows here
just the stark insinuation of desire
of objects and their absence